STAR WARS

2 CLASSICS FROM A GALAXY FAR, FAR AWAY...
MUSIC BY JOHN WILLIAMS

Arranged by Phillip Keveren

— PIANO LEVEL —
ADVANCED

ISBN 978-1-4950-8352-5

DISTRIBUTED BY

HAL•LEONARD®

7777 W. BLUEMOUND RD. P.O. BOX 13819 MILWAUKEE, WI 53213

In Australia Contact:
Hal Leonard Australia Pty. Ltd.
4 Lentara Court
Cheltenham, Victoria, 3192 Australia
Email: ausadmin@halleonard.com.au

Visit Hal Leonard Online at
www.halleonard.com

Visit Phillip at
www.phillipkeveren.com

PREFACE

It was the summer of 1977 and my family was on vacation in southern California. My cousin and I stood in line for hours, waiting for what was that season's breakout blockbuster: *Star Wars*. The theatre was cavernous, the type of venue rarely seen today, where 2,000 people could share in movie magic simultaneously. When the lights dimmed and John Williams's now-famous fanfare filled the space, my musical sensibilities were forever altered. It was not long after that first screening that I purchased the soundtrack – on LP, of course! – and began my lifelong love affair with this great music.

So, it is with this personal history that I approached the collection of piano arrangements you now hold. I hope I was able to maintain a balance between staying true to Williams's original orchestral aspirations and the desire to make each arrangement a unique and fulfilling piano solo.

May the Force be with you – and watch the fingerings… and don't over-pedal!

Phillip Keveren

BIOGRAPHY

Phillip Keveren, a multi-talented keyboard artist and composer, has composed original works in a variety of genres from piano solo to symphonic orchestra. Mr. Keveren gives frequent concerts and workshops for teachers and their students in the United States, Canada, Europe, and Asia. Mr. Keveren holds a B.M. in composition from California State University Northridge and a M.M. in composition from the University of Southern California.

CONTENTS

4   **ACROSS THE STARS**

8   **BATTLE OF THE HEROES**

16 **CANTINA BAND**

20 **DUEL OF THE FATES**

13 **THE IMPERIAL MARCH (DARTH VADER'S THEME)**

24 **LUKE AND LEIA**

30 *MARCH OF THE RESISTANCE*

35 **PRINCESS LEIA'S THEME**

38 **REY'S THEME**

43 **STAR WARS (MAIN THEME)**

46 **THE THRONE ROOM *AND* FINALE**

49 **YODA'S THEME**

ACROSS THE STARS
(Love Theme from STAR WARS: ATTACK OF THE CLONES)

Music by JOHN WILLIAMS
Arranged by Phillip Keveren

BATTLE OF THE HEROES

From STAR WARS: REVENGE OF THE SITH

Music by JOHN WILLIAMS
Arranged by Phillip Keveren

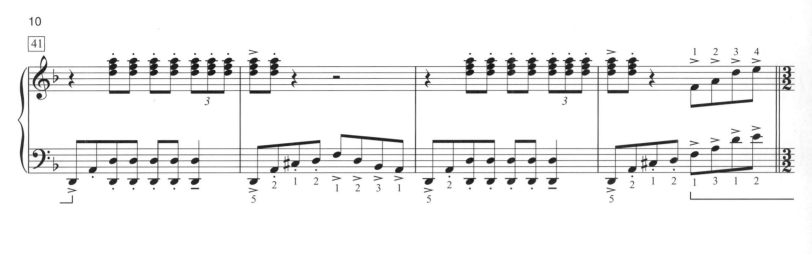

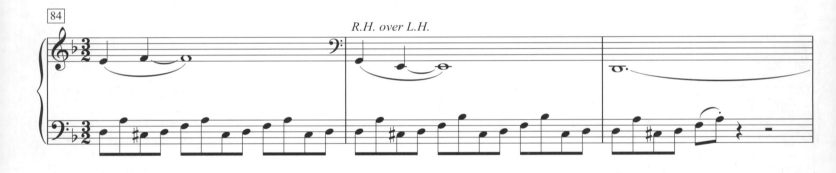

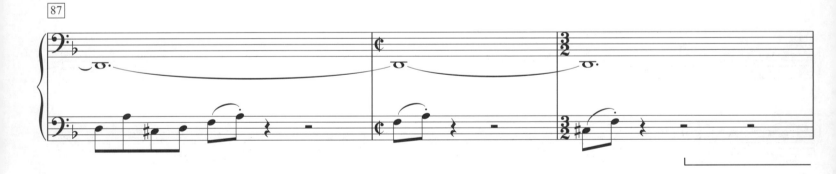

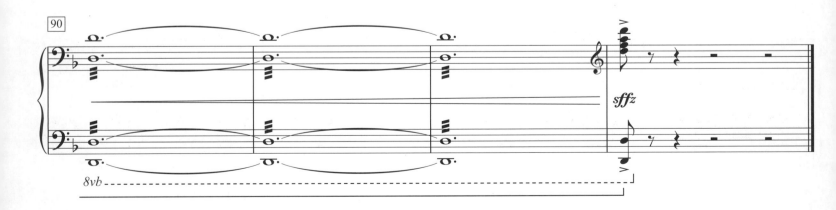

THE IMPERIAL MARCH
(Darth Vader's Theme)
From STAR WARS: THE EMPIRE STRIKES BACK

Music by JOHN WILLIAMS
Arranged by Phillip Keveren

CANTINA BAND

From STAR WARS: A NEW HOPE

Music by JOHN WILLIAMS
Arranged by Phillip Keveren

With Old-Time Jazz-Band Zeal (♩ = 132)

DUEL OF THE FATES
From STAR WARS: THE PHANTOM MENACE

Music by JOHN WILLIAMS
Arranged by Phillip Keveren

LUKE AND LEIA
From STAR WARS: RETURN OF THE JEDI

Music by JOHN WILLIAMS
Arranged by Phillip Keveren

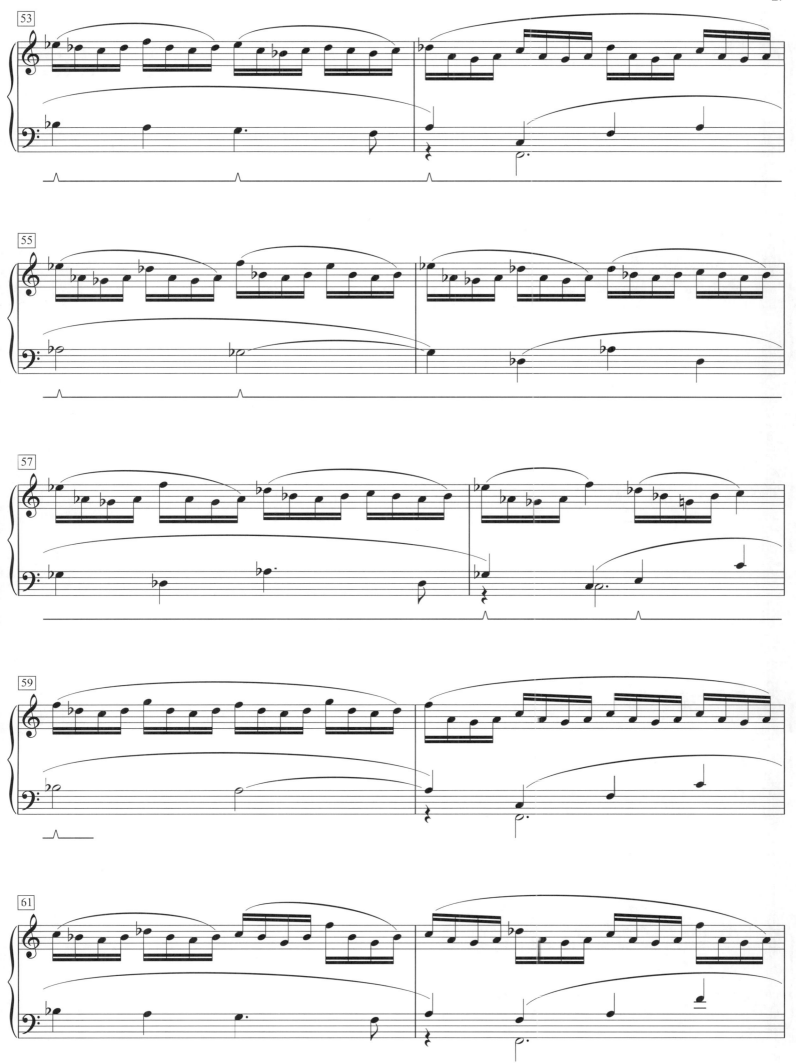

MARCH OF THE RESISTANCE

From STAR WARS: THE FORCE AWAKENS

Music by JOHN WILLIAMS
Arranged by Phillip Keveren

PRINCESS LEIA'S THEME

From STAR WARS: A NEW HOPE

Music by JOHN WILLIAMS
Arranged by Phillip Keveren

Cantabile (♩ = c. 60)

REY'S THEME

From STAR WARS: THE FORCE AWAKENS

Music by JOHN WILLIAMS
Arranged by Phillip Keveren

STAR WARS
(Main Theme)
From STAR WARS: A NEW HOPE

Music by JOHN WILLIAMS
Arranged by Phillip Keveren

THE THRONE ROOM *AND* FINALE

From STAR WARS: A NEW HOPE

Music by JOHN WILLIAMS
Arranged by Phillip Keveren

YODA'S THEME

From STAR WARS: THE EMPIRE STRIKES BACK

Music by JOHN WILLIAMS
Arranged by Phillip Keveren

Cantabile, with rubato (♩ = c. 80)

THE PHILLIP KEVEREN SERIES

PIANO SOLO

00156644	ABBA for Classical Piano	$15.99
00311024	Above All	$12.99
00311348	Americana	$12.99
00198473	Bach Meets Jazz	$14.99
00313594	Bacharach and David	$15.99
00306412	The Beatles	$17.99
00312189	The Beatles for Classical Piano	$16.99
00275876	The Beatles – Recital Suites	$19.99
00312546	Best Piano Solos	$15.99
00156601	Blessings	$12.99
00198656	Blues Classics	$12.99
00284359	Broadway Songs with a Classical Flair	$14.99
00310669	Broadway's Best	$14.99
00312106	Canzone Italiana	$12.99
00280848	Carpenters	$16.99
00310629	A Celtic Christmas	$12.99
00310549	The Celtic Collection	$12.95
00280571	Celtic Songs with a Classical Flair	$12.99
00263362	Charlie Brown Favorites	$14.99
00312190	Christmas at the Movies	$14.99
00294754	Christmas Carols with a Classical Flair	$12.99
00311414	Christmas Medleys	$14.99
00236669	Christmas Praise Hymns	$12.99
00233788	Christmas Songs for Classical Piano	$12.99
00311769	Christmas Worship Medleys	$14.99
00310607	Cinema Classics	$15.99
00301857	Circles	$10.99
00311101	Classic Wedding Songs	$10.95
00311292	Classical Folk	$10.95
00311083	Classical Jazz	$12.95
00137779	Coldplay for Classical Piano	$16.99
00311103	Contemporary Wedding Songs	$12.99
00348788	Country Songs with a Classical Flair	$14.99
00249097	Disney Recital Suites	$17.99
00311754	Disney Songs for Classical Piano	$17.99
00241379	Disney Songs for Ragtime Piano	$17.99
00311881	Favorite Wedding Songs	$14.99
00315974	Fiddlin' at the Piano	$12.99
00311811	The Film Score Collection	$15.99
00269408	Folksongs with a Classical Flair	$12.99
00144353	The Gershwin Collection	$14.99
00233789	Golden Scores	$14.99
00144351	Gospel Greats	$12.99
00183566	The Great American Songbook	$12.99
00312084	The Great Melodies	$12.99
00311157	Great Standards	$12.95
00171621	A Grown-Up Christmas List	$12.99
00311071	The Hymn Collection	$12.99
00311349	Hymn Medleys	$12.99

00280705	Hymns in a Celtic Style	$12.99
00269407	Hymns with a Classical Flair	$12.99
00311249	Hymns with a Touch of Jazz	$12.99
00310905	I Could Sing of Your Love Forever	$12.95
00310762	Jingle Jazz	$14.99
00175310	Billy Joel for Classical Piano	$16.99
00126449	Elton John for Classical Piano	$16.99
00310839	Let Freedom Ring!	$12.99
00238988	Andrew Lloyd Webber Piano Songbook	$14.99
00313227	Andrew Lloyd Webber Solos	$15.99
00313523	Mancini Magic	$16.99
00312113	More Disney Songs for Classical Piano	$16.99
00311295	Motown Hits	$14.99
00300640	Piano Calm	$12.99
00339131	Piano Calm: Christmas	$12.99
00346009	Piano Calm: Prayer	$14.99
00306870	Piazzolla Tangos	$16.99
00156645	Queen for Classical Piano	$15.99
00310755	Richard Rodgers Classics	$16.99
00289545	Scottish Songs	$12.99
00310609	Shout to the Lord!	$14.99
00119403	The Sound of Music	$14.99
00311978	The Spirituals Collection	$10.99
00210445	Star Wars	$16.99
00224738	Symphonic Hymns for Piano	$14.99
00279673	Tin Pan Alley	$12.99
00312112	Treasured Hymns for Classical Piano	$14.99
00144926	The Twelve Keys of Christmas	$12.99
00278486	The Who for Classical Piano	$16.99
00294036	Worship with a Touch of Jazz	$12.99
00311911	Yuletide Jazz	$17.99

EASY PIANO

00210401	Adele for Easy Classical Piano	$15.99
00310610	African-American Spirituals	$10.99
00218244	The Beatles for Easy Classical Piano	$14.99
00218387	Catchy Songs for Piano	$12.99
00310973	Celtic Dreams	$12.99
00233686	Christmas Carols for Easy Classical Piano	$12.99
00311126	Christmas Pops	$14.99
00311548	Classic Pop/Rock Hits	$14.99
00310769	A Classical Christmas	$10.95
00310975	Classical Movie Themes	$12.99
00144352	Disney Songs for Easy Classical Piano	$12.99
00311093	Early Rock 'n' Roll	$14.99
00311997	Easy Worship Medleys	$12.99
00289547	Duke Ellington	$14.99
00160297	Folksongs for Easy Classical Piano	$12.99

00110374	George Gershwin Classics	$12.99
00310805	Gospel Treasures	$12.99
00306821	Vince Guaraldi Collection	$19.99
00160294	Hymns for Easy Classical Piano	$12.99
00310798	Immortal Hymns	$12.99
00311294	Jazz Standards	$12.99
00310744	Love Songs	$12.99
00233740	The Most Beautiful Songs for Easy Classical Piano	$12.99
00220036	Pop Ballads	$14.99
00311406	Pop Gems of the 1950s	$12.95
00311407	Pop Gems of the 1960s	$12.95
00233739	Pop Standards for Easy Classical Piano	$12.99
00102887	A Ragtime Christmas	$12.99
00311293	Ragtime Classics	$10.95
00312028	Santa Swings	$12.99
00233688	Songs from Childhood for Easy Classical Piano	$12.99
00103258	Songs of Inspiration	$12.99
00310840	Sweet Land of Liberty	$12.99
00126450	10,000 Reasons	$14.99
00310712	Timeless Praise	$12.95
00311086	TV Themes	$12.99
00310717	21 Great Classics	$12.99
00160076	Waltzes & Polkas for Easy Classical Piano	$12.99
00145342	Weekly Worship	$16.99

BIG-NOTE PIANO

00310838	Children's Favorite Movie Songs	$12.99
00346000	Christmas Movie Magic	$12.99
00277368	Classical Favorites	$12.99
00310907	Contemporary Hits	$12.99
00277370	Disney Favorites	$14.99
00310888	Joy to the World	$12.99
00310908	The Nutcracker	$12.99
00277371	Star Wars	$16.99

BEGINNING PIANO SOLOS

00311202	Awesome God	$12.99
00310837	Christian Children's Favorites	$12.99
00311117	Christmas Traditions	$10.99
00311250	Easy Hymns	$12.99
00102710	Everlasting God	$10.99
00311403	Jazzy Tunes	$10.95
00310822	Kids' Favorites	$12.99
00338175	Silly Songs for Kids	$9.99

PIANO DUET

00126452	The Christmas Variations	$12.99
00311350	Classical Theme Duets	$10.99
00295099	Gospel Duets	$12.99
00311544	Hymn Duets	$14.99
00311203	Praise & Worship Duets	$12.99
00294755	Sacred Christmas Duets	$12.99
00119405	Star Wars	$14.99
00253545	Worship Songs for Two	$12.99

*Prices, contents, and availability
subject to change without notice.*

0221

158